ORGANIZATIONS THAT HELP THE WORLD

WORLD WIDE FUND FOR NATURE

PETER DENTON

OTHER TITLES IN THE SERIES
Amnesty International by Marsha Bronson (1-85015-307-8)
Greenpeace by Paul Brown (1-85015-366-3)
The Red Cross and the Red Crescent by Michael Pollard (1-85015-305-1)
United Nations High Commission for Refugees by Jean Trier (1-85015-365-5)
United Nations by Michael Pollard (1-85015-306-X)

Picture credits:
Gamma: 11 (bottom); **Greenpeace UK:** 7 (bottom); **Images Colour Library:** 56 (bottom); **Image Select:** 14, 15, 29 (bottom); **Jacana:** 28; **WWF Gland (Switzerland):** 5, 6 (bottom), 8 (all), 9, 10/11, 13 (top), 17, 18, 21 (top and margin), 27 (bottom), 31 (both), 32, 33 (bottom), 36 (both), 37, 38, 39 (bottom), 42, 43, 44, 45 (all), 51, 54, 55, 56 (top), 57 (both), 58, 59 (all), 60; **WWF UK:** cover, 6 (top), 7, (top), 12 (all), 13 (bottom), 16 (both), 19 (both), 20, 21, (bottom left), 23 (both), 24 (both), 25, 26, 27 (top), 29 (top), 33 (top), 34 (both), 35, 39 (top), 40/41, 41 (both), 47, 48/49, 49, 52/53; **Zefa:** 4.

Special thanks to Michèle Dépraz and Rachel Catelano for their help on picture research.

Published in Great Britain in 1993
by Exley Publications Ltd,
16 Chalk Hill, Watford,
Herts WD1 4BN, United Kingdom.

Copyright © Exley Publications, 1993
Text copyright © Peter Denton, 1993
Reprinted 1995

A copy of the CIP data is available from the British Library on request.

ISBN 1-85015-367-1

All rights reserved. No part of this publication may be reproduced or transmitted in any form or by any means, electronic or mechanical, including photocopy, recording or any information storage and retrieval system without permission in writing from the Publisher.

Series editor: Helen Exley
Editor: Samantha Armstrong
Editorial Assistant: Helen Lanz
Research: Margaret Montgomery
Picture research: Alex Goldberg and James Clift of Image Select
Typeset by Delta Print, Watford, Herts, UK
Printed by Kossuth Printing House Co. in Hungary

WORLD WIDE FUND FOR NATURE

PETER DENTON

◪EXLEY

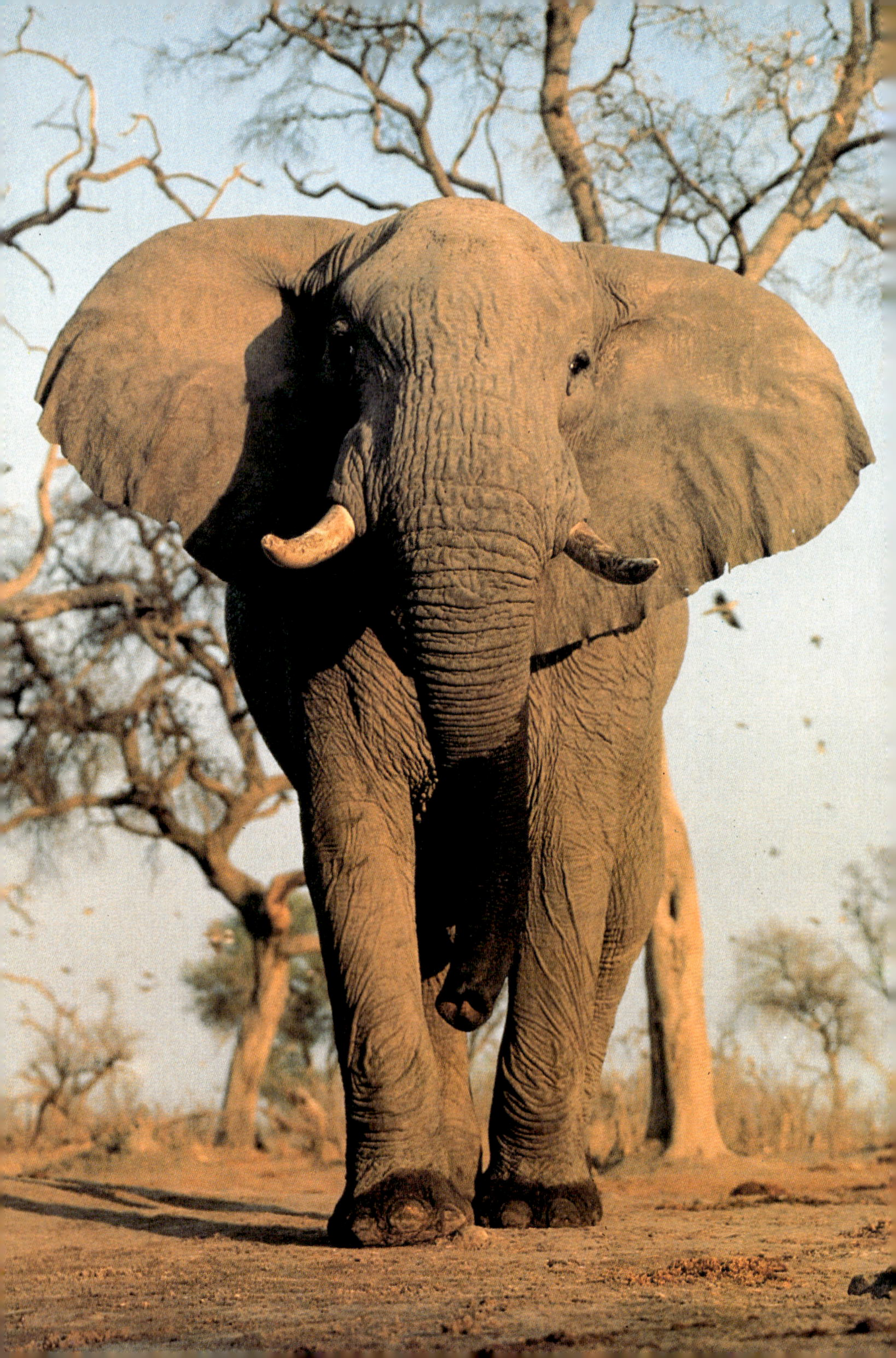

Human greed

Crack! A shot rings out. Then another. And another. For a moment, silence.

Then, the most dreadful noise. A deafening, frightening trumpeting, followed by the sounds of breaking branches, tearing undergrowth, crashing bushes and the crushing of young trees.

Five tonnes of bone, muscle and flesh have just been stopped dead in their tracks. Another elephant literally hits the dust – murdered for its tusks which weigh, in comparison, a mere forty kilograms.

But this is no extraordinary event. Every year, as many as seventy thousand elephants are killed in Africa by poachers greedy for profits from the sale of ivory. The bulls have the best tusks, but who cares whether the animals are adolescent, in their prime or old? Ivory means money so kill them.

Elephants' tusks can be up to three metres long and are virtually solid for two-thirds of their length. They

Above and opposite: From this magnificent elephant to this array of tusks. Twelve tonnes of ivory lie before Kenyan authorities who confiscated it in the late 1980s. The estimated yearly trade was five thousand tusks shortly before this mass confiscation.

Below: Killed for ivory, half of Africa's elephants were wiped out in the 1970s and 1980s. Top and opposite top: During the early 1980s, research showed that four to six million carved ivory products were imported into world markets. The declared value of this and the seized tusks was US$20 million to US$30 million. Opposite bottom: In an effort to diminish the economic value of ivory, poached ivory that has been confiscated is burned. However, as elephant herds have to be culled for their own survival, some ivory is sold legally with profits helping the country.

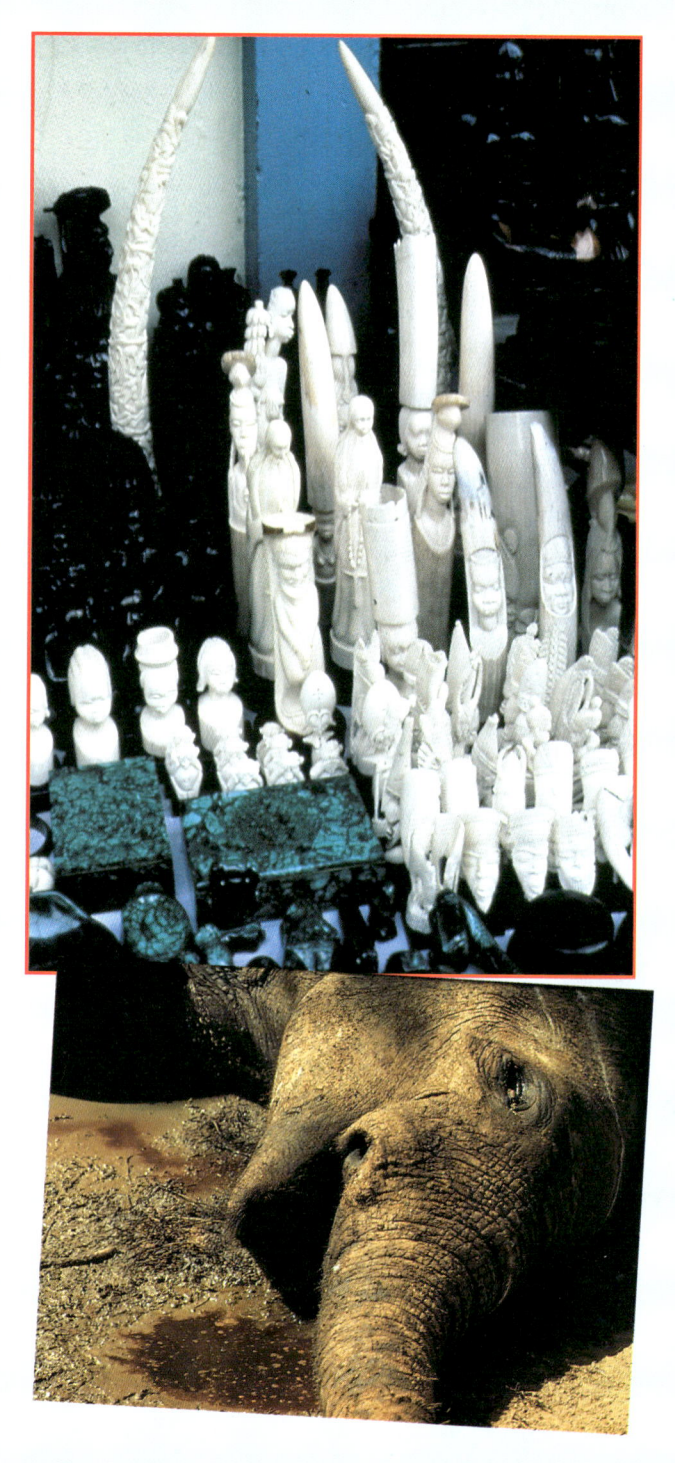

grow as the elephant grows and an elephant can live, if allowed to, from fifty to seventy years. These illegally poached tusks are carved up, etched into delicately intricate designs, polished and sold as trinkets, keyrings, ornaments and necklaces that can easily be bought in the backstreet markets of Asia.

These are decades of destruction; in 1973, fifty-five thousand elephants were slaughtered for one thousand tonnes of ivory; in 1983, one hundred thousand elephants were killed for exactly the same amount. In order to get that much ivory every year, poachers kill female and young elephants and destroy carefully managed herds.

This is just part of the story about the plundering of the animal kingdom by human beings. The story involves the destruction of the habitats in which animals, birds, fish and humans live. It is about the terrible damage being done to the water we drink and the air we breathe.

This is a story about the slow and unnecessary death of the earth and why the world needs an international environmental organization to try to halt that destruction. WWF, World Wide Fund For Nature, is just such an organization.

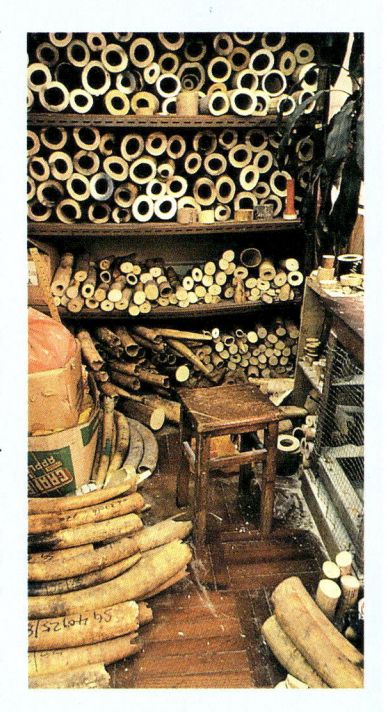

WWF's mission

WWF is one of the world's largest and most influential international nature conservation organizations. It has over three million members who raise money to tackle issues such as pollution, the survival of all species and global warming – issues that cross international boundaries, cultures and beliefs.

WWF has no political bias. It has offices in all five continents and branches in over forty countries. It brings people together in a unified cause.

WWF's reason for being is simple ... but complex. It distributes funds and campaigns to preserve the incredible variety of life on earth. It educates humankind to use natural resources, like water, timber and fish stocks – which can renew themselves if given a chance – in ways that do not exhaust supplies. And it aims to reduce pollution and the wasteful consumption of resources and energy to a minimum.

A protection plan for the world

WWF's wildlife protection plan covers all species whether endangered or not – from whales, insects and elephants to rhinos, amphibians and monkeys.

It works to conserve all flora and fauna, oceans and coasts, rivers and lakes, landscapes, air and soils.

It researches into, and campaigns for, well-managed agricultural and transport policies. It researches into, and campaigns against, damage to the ozone layer and pollution in the air, on land and in the seas and watercourses. It aims to protect habitats and to create reserves that ensure species survive.

WWF promotes the idea of people living in harmony with their natural surroundings. Its ultimate goal is to stop, and eventually reverse, the fast-growing ruination of the planet's natural environment. To reach that goal, the organization has developed a series of action plans that will take it through to the twenty-first century.

WWF believes there is no time to spare on any of these issues.

How it all began

In 1960, the decline in the number of animals in western Africa was dramatic.

At that time, the United Nations' advisor on wildlife conservation was one of the world's most distinguished zoologists and biologists, Sir Julian Huxley. He made some observations in Africa that led him to warn the world that much of Africa's wildlife could be extinct within twenty years.

"Many parts [of Africa] which, fifty years ago, were swarming with game are now bare of wildlife," he cautioned. "Cultivation is extending, native cattle are multiplying at the expense of wild animals, poaching is becoming heavier and more organized, forests are being cut down and destroyed."

Coming from such an eminent zoologist, the warnings were grave and dire but "conservation" was a subject few people, other than animal experts, thought about in the early 1960s.

But, even so, Sir Julian Huxley's warning was taken

seriously. He received many letters, including one from a business executive, Victor Stolan. If African wildlife were to be saved, Stolan wrote, "vigorous and immediate" fund-raising on an international scale would need to be organized.

This letter stood out from the rest because it came up with a positive and totally new idea: raising money to save wildlife. Sir Julian Huxley took note.

The weeks that followed were busy. Telephones rang, letters were written, ears bent, hands shaken and consciences stirred.

Sir Peter Scott

Not least among the people consulted was Peter Scott, the son of the famous Antarctic explorer, Captain Robert Falcon Scott. Peter Scott was a notable ornithologist and naturalist. He was also a vice-president of the International Union for the Conservation of Nature and Natural Resources (IUCN). Sir Julian Huxley was also involved with this organization, being one of the IUCN's founder members.

The IUCN, now known as the World Conservation Union, provides leadership and scientific expertise in the field of world conservation. It monitors natural resources and how they are used throughout the world. It analyzes the problems of conservation and how to solve them without damaging the traditions of local communities. Today, WWF and the World Conservation Union also make people aware of the huge conservation issues at stake if species, including the human species, are to survive.

But in the 1950s and early 1960s the IUCN did not have funds to spend on its projects. On its behalf, Peter Scott said he would be interested in discussing the idea of fund-raising for nature.

A deal is struck

Being a scientific organization, the IUCN did not have the capability to raise money – but it did have a brilliant array of scientific knowledge, as well as research projects across the world.

So a handful of representatives of the proposal

Pictured in their natural environment, the tree frog (opposite top), the golden lion tamarin (opposite middle), the hawksbill turtle (opposite bottom) and the chimpanzee. It is the habitat of these animals that WWF and other conservation organizations are striving to protect.

A giant panda balances precariously as it searches for its staple food, bamboo. In the mid-eighties, 90% of the bamboo food stocks in the Wolong reserve area died, putting the panda population at great risk.

*In 1988 the World Wildlife Fund changed its name to World Wide Fund For Nature except in Canada and the United States of America where it remained the same.

presented the organization with an interesting offer: they would raise money to finance projects, if the IUCN would share its research. They would also make representations to senior levels of government – using famous people to help them gain access – to save wildlife.

It seemed like a great partnership. The World Wildlife Fund (known as the World Wide Fund For Nature since 1988) was on its way. But it needed its own special logo to make it easily identifiable.

Finding a logo

At about this time, record numbers of visitors were flocking to London Zoo to see a very rare resident: a giant panda, named Chi-Chi.

She had been bought by an animal dealer in China on

Below: Two of a kind. This photograph is rare as it is extremely unusual for pandas to give birth to twins and normally, only one will survive. Mothers hug their cubs tightly and protect them for the first eighteen months of their lives.

behalf of an American zoo, but political relations between China and the United States were so bad at the time that the Americans branded the panda "Communist goods" and banned her from entering their country. So she was bought by London Zoo in 1958 and became the star attraction.

Among the thousands of visitors to the zoo was a naturalist named Gerald Watterson. He drew some rough sketches of Chi-Chi at play – standing up, rolling over, lying down, sitting on her haunches and resting. She was big, cuddly, very furry and, because of the black patches on her face, seemed to have large, appealing eyes. For these reasons, and because the species was in great danger of becoming extinct, the giant panda was the obvious choice for the logo that would represent the new WWF organization.

From Watterson's sketches, Peter Scott designed the

panda logo – a very simple black and white drawing that could be reproduced easily and cheaply. It was to become one of the most famous logos of any group in the world.

Meanwhile, in Morges, Switzerland, the IUCN held a special meeting to discuss the immediate threat to the world's wildlife.

Sir Julian Huxley and Peter Scott were among the delegates who were appalled at the senseless killing of animals that was going unchecked throughout the world. They, and fourteen other leading conservationists from Europe, Africa and the United States, signed a plea to the world.

This urgent appeal became known as the Morges Manifesto. It was notable not only for its important message, but for its straightforward language. The Manifesto set down the very reasons why an organization, like WWF, was so badly needed.

This declaration set people talking all over the world. For WWF, its timing could hardly have been better – until then, anyone supporting the conservation movement was regarded as being "way out"; most people neither knew nor cared about the growing pace of wildlife and habitat destruction.

WWF is launched

If any new organization is to succeed, it needs publicity and money more than anything else. If people don't know about it, they cannot support it.

The launch of WWF made news across the world: it was, after all, the first international organization that pledged to save endangered wildlife on a world-wide scale.

But publicity can fade quickly and there's nothing so old as yesterday's news. WWF's public relations expert, Ian MacPhail, knew this maxim well. He invited one of Britain's most popular newspapers, the *Daily Mirror,* to become the first newspaper in the world to tell its readers how severely some animals were at risk; not through natural causes, but because of human greed and ignorance.

Headline news

Monday, October 9, 1961. That morning, four-and-a-half million readers had never seen anything like it. "DOOMED – TO DISAPPEAR FROM THE FACE OF THE EARTH DUE TO MAN'S FOLLY, GREED, NEGLECT" was the newspaper's front page headline. A large picture showed Gertie, a rhinoceros with a freak horn more than a metre long, shortly before she was killed by poachers.

The seven-page article told its readers that because of the "thoughtless foolishness of the most superior animal on earth – Man himself" – the Galapagos giant tortoise, the Asian Bactrian camel, the Indian elephant and the North American whooping crane were among the creatures on an extinction danger list.

The *Mirror* spoke of a "twentieth century death flood" and described WWF as a "world crusade". And it added: "This crusade needs YOUR support. If you don't want the phrase 'dead as a dodo' to be replaced by 'dead as a rhino', read on."

Readers read on. They also dug into their pockets. Within seven days the British readers had donated more than £60,000 to WWF – the equivalent of nearly three quarters of a million pounds today.

First projects

With this money, WWF was quickly established as an international organization and it set up headquarters in the politically neutral country of Switzerland. But it needed to be represented in as many countries as possible so that its message could be heard loud and clear.

Within six weeks, WWF national organizations were set up in four countries. Now there are twenty-eight WWF national organizations around the world and all are independent of each other, although they are constantly in touch about common issues. They raise funds and run projects in their own countries and, in addition, the wealthier ones contribute around two-thirds of their income to WWF conservation schemes outside their territories. Money is raised through membership fees, by selling gifts, from donations, by allowing the use of the panda logo on different products and by members

The Tasmanian wolf (above) is now thought to be extinct in Tasmania. By the early part of the century it was already rare as a result of hunting, the destruction of its forest habitat and an epidemic that decimated the population.

Opposite: The WWF logo was inspired by these sketches of Chi-Chi the giant panda, drawn by Gerald Watterson in 1961. The organization's current logo (below) is the final result.

In the days of the British Empire, King George V was also Emperor of India. During the rule of the British in India, tiger-hunting increased dramatically – not only as a sport but also to protect the village settlements. Here, the king treks out on the back of an elephant for a day's shooting for pleasure.

standing on street corners shaking cans.

One of the first projects funded by WWF was for a footpath with signboards in the Ambato Malamo forest reserve in Madagascar: this was to keep the destruction of the forest areas by people to a minimum. It also gave money to help the transportation of eight endangered white rhinos from South Africa to Southern Rhodesia (now Zimbabwe) for breeding, as well as funding the capture of three very rare Arabian oryx in Aden (now Yemen) for breeding in specialized zoos – a project that saved the species from extinction.

Bigger projects

In 1972, WWF launched its largest and most extensive campaign so far: "Operation Tiger". It would try to save the tiger and its habitat. Some one hundred thousand tigers roamed the wild in Asia in 1920. By 1972, there were only five thousand surviving.

On the Indian sub-continent, the numbers were just as alarming. In 1969, there were only 2,500 left from an original forty thousand seventy years before. The IUCN immediately called on its members to meet in order to discuss the tiger's fate.

King George V inspects the spoils of his day's entertainment. As the Indian population grew during the 1800s so more land was required for agriculture to feed the people; this meant that more tigers were displaced as their natural habitat was destroyed. Many tigers became man-eaters as their usual prey was killed by humans.

How could numbers fall so rapidly? Largely because of the human desire to kill. Rich colonial rulers, maharajas, visiting royalty, explorers and tourists formed shooting parties and headed into the jungle for a good day's "sport", hunting the "viceroy's tiger", so called because it was bigger than other breeds. It was not uncommon for a single group to bag two or three tigers in a day. King George V of Great Britain and the Maharaja of Nepal shot thirty-nine tigers in eleven days in a shooting party in 1911. The Raja of Gwalior was said to have shot as many as seven hundred tigers in his lifetime.

But, while many people today regard big game hunting as objectionable, it was completely acceptable in the first part of this century. It was thought to be a fine example of human skill against the deadly animal. Magazines published photographs of wealthy hunters posing proudly in front of a dead tiger hanging upside down on a pole borne by servants.

"Tigers lived for hundreds of thousands of years in an ocean of forests, heavily populated with prey, where people existed in small numbers in isolated groups...Now it is the tigers that live isolated in small numbers. An ocean of people has replaced the ocean of trees and is pressing in on the remaining islands of tiger habitat."

Peter Jackson, from "Endangered Species - Tigers".

Opposite: A magnificent Bengal tiger. A dead tiger can fetch as much as US$15,000 and there have even been reports that tigers have been exchanged for luxury goods, including cars. Below: Every tiger has unique markings on its face and head. This sedated tiger has its photograph taken for official records. Below right: Having been given a mild sedative, a collar is fitted. The tiger must be constantly cooled with water as the sedative can raise its body temperature to dangerous levels.

"Project Tiger"

Times and attitudes gradually changed and by mid-1971 there was a total ban on tiger hunting in all the Indian states. A census in India indicated that there were just 1,800 Bengal tigers left in the country. A WWF team saw India's prime minister, Mrs. Indira Gandhi, who immediately promised official action.

Within a few months, under Mrs. Gandhi's personal supervision, the Indian government initiated a six year conservation plan, "Project Tiger", with financial support from WWF. Nine reserves were established where the animals could roam undisturbed and without fear of hunters' guns.

Tracking the tigers

Before long, other WWF grants enabled Thailand and Indonesia to set up or improve havens for their own tigers. The WWF money was used, in the main, for research work and supplies. It provided four-wheel drive jeeps, motorcycles, cameras, night-vision scopes, two-way radios, speed boats for patrolling the rivers and swamps, office equipment, binoculars and laboratory supplies.

Miniature radio transmitters were supplied to enable wardens to keep track of the tigers. In order to fit these tiny radios, the animals had to be drugged. The wardens and WWF staff then moved in and fitted collars with transmitters onto the animals. When the tigers woke, they were unaware of the operation having taken place. From that moment, wherever they were, their mini-radios sent out signals which enabled wardens to know exactly where they were living, how far they moved every day, how much space each tiger occupied, how they divided their living areas up so that each tiger had a big enough area to hunt in and whether they were heading for known danger spots.

Over the years the Indian government has put the equivalent of more than US$30 million into its tiger conservation project which still continues. In Nepal, the government set up a reserve, the Chitwan National Park, and WWF funded its first full-scale research plan into the tiger's environment.

The then Indian prime minister, Indira Gandhi, tenderly holds a tiger cub in 1973. Mrs. Gandhi was one of the first international leaders to join the crusade to save endangered species.

The Indian government, with advice from WWF experts, soon realized that there was more to saving the tiger than just banning the act of deliberate killing.

The tiger had to be given a good chance of survival and this would also involve looking after its habitat – the wide area where it lived, hunted and slept. The saving of the environment had to be considered as equally important.

This meant that tree felling had to be reduced so that the tigers would have cover. The undergrowth also had to be protected, as well as rivers, streams and all the animals, like deer, upon which the tigers preyed. To survive, one tiger needs one hundred large prey every year. So a reserve with five hundred tigers in it would need fifty thousand animals for the tiger to prey on. No food? No tigers.

Establishing and clearing the reserves needed to be done with care. In some cases, people had lived for generations in the nine areas that had been designated as reserves. Great sensitivity was necessary if the people were to be re-settled successfully and their villages re-built elsewhere.

This was achieved with surprisingly little disruption; people were settled in new areas where houses were built for them and the land already prepared for their arrival. Schools, temples and clinics were also built for the new areas. The scheme quickly became a major success with no less than eighteen special reserves eventually being established.

Once relieved of the drain of human farming, grazing livestock and the felling of trees for fuel, the natural vegetation of the areas soon recovered. In some areas, dams were built to provide pools for the tigers to drink at and to swim in.

By 1980, the number of tigers had increased to three thousand and by 1990 there were believed to be as many as four thousand. Things were looking good. But not for long: poachers were at work.

Despite the great efforts and achievements of WWF in conjunction with the Indian government and other interested countries, the tiger again became one of the most endangered species on earth.

Ironically, the very success of "Project Tiger" and "Operation Tiger" was in part responsible: there were so many animals that they became easy to spot. That was great for the thousands of tourists who visited the reserves every year, but it also made the tigers easy targets for poachers.

Killing for profit

All too many rare animals fall victim to poachers: people who kill or trap animals against their own country's laws. They might kill for food, or as a way of earning money, or even for "fun".

Poaching can range from killing a deer in order to provide meat or a modest income for a family, to persecuting small animals, such as badgers, for human entertainment, to shooting an endangered black rhino for its horn.

Killing methods vary greatly and death is not always instant. Many poachers cannot afford guns or bullets, so they use poisons, snares, traps, knives or machetes. Often the creatures are left to die slowly and, usually, in terrible pain.

Poachers who go for big wildlife usually operate with large guns. Once the victim has been felled and killed, a saw will be brought in to carve up and remove the parts that are valuable: a tusk or a rhino horn, for example. Whatever is not wanted is left to scavenging birds and animals.

Monkey brains for medicines

For thousands of years in many parts of Asia, people have believed that drinking specially-prepared medicines, containing powdered-down parts of animals, can cure all manner of ailments, such as rheumatism and arthritis. Others believe that taking the concoctions will help them live longer. So, for many reasons, tiger bones, rhino horns, bear gall bladders and monkey brains are still much in demand.

The black rhinoceros is on the verge of extinction because its horn is made into drinking cups and knife handles. There is also a strong belief in some parts of the world that rhino horn acts as a painkiller, curing all kinds of disorders including fever and skin ulcers. Leopards, tigers and other great cats are shamelessly

Exotic birds often have their bright feathers dyed black in order to be smuggled from the country of origin.

killed for their skins that end up draped around human bodies as fur coats.

Whales – the largest and most gentle mammals in the world – are killed because some people, most notably in Japan, regard whale meat as a great delicacy for which they are prepared to pay enormous sums of money in smart restaurants.

For sale

In other cases, wild creatures are worth more money alive than dead. Elaborate traps are set to capture animals and birds without damaging them. Once caught, they will be bound, drugged, hooded, then dumped into sacks or crates and transported in gruesome discomfort to parts of the world where they are in demand. There, they will be chained up or caged and sold for huge profits.

Beautiful birds, monkeys, reptiles and rare plants are openly for sale in the street markets of Thailand, Vietnam, Hong Kong, Laos and Taiwan. From there, they are illegally re-shipped to new destinations – anywhere in the world where individuals are willing to pay handsomely.

Stopping the poachers

In 1976, WWF set up an organization called the Trade Records Analysis of Flora and Fauna in Commerce, TRAFFIC, to put an end to this trade.

TRAFFIC is the largest wildlife trade monitoring scheme in the world, observing, recording and investigating the illegal buying and selling of endangered species. This means that some operations have to be undercover.

TRAFFIC staff travel worldwide to track down sources of illegal wildlife trading and sometimes it can be risky. "If you spend a lot of time nosing around customs sheds and docks, you are bound to run into some unsavoury characters," says Jørgen Thomsen, who heads the TRAFFIC team. "We are really in the same position as drugs enforcement officers and sometimes we're up against huge vested criminal interests."

While major trading interests are operating, so, too,

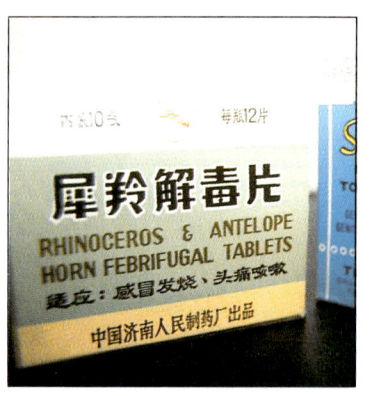

The end of the line. Rhinoceros and antelope horn is smuggled to China, where it is ground down and made into tablets for human consumption. In Taiwan, the price of rhino horn almost quadrupled between 1985 and 1993. This was due, in part, to the belief that the rhino's extinction is imminent.

"If people refused to buy ivory carving, rhino horn, rare parrots, spotted cat fur coats, reptile skin goods ... or rare cacti or orchids and the like, the trade in endangered species would rapidly dry up."

From "Atlas of the Environment", a WWF publication.

Despite being illegal, products such as these lizard leg keyrings, tiger skin rugs or tortoiseshell guitars are still available in countries such as Indonesia, Thailand and Morocco.

Opposite top: Tourists gather to see the dancing bear in Turkey...this bear is muzzled and forced to "dance" to the sound of a tambourine. This is one of the most shocking examples of the cruel exploitation of animals by humans.

Opposite below: A terrified white-headed gibbon is offered for sale by a market trader in Bangkok. Despite there being sufficient laws to put a stop to at least 90% of illegal trade such as this, they are so difficult for the authorities to enforce, that a blind eye is often turned to the plight of the animals.

are many individuals who work for their own gain or for private "clients". Large or small, they are monitored by TRAFFIC.

Smuggling involves big money. Such large amounts, in fact, that estimates place the illegal trade in wildlife and plants third after drug dealing and the arms trade.

Success

In Malawi, TRAFFIC investigators, working with the local and South African police, exposed an ivory smuggling operation. They apprehended three people carrying seventy-eight elephant tusks, many of which were taken from young elephants believed to have been shot in Malawi's Thuma Forest Reserve.

Baboons, marmosets, tortoises and parrots were recently found on a Russian ship; two hundred Indian star tortoises were intercepted in the Netherlands en route from Dubai to the United States; and, in China, a man was jailed for twelve years after he tried to sell a panda skin in Shanghai.

In Italy, three chimpanzees were seized from a circus after TRAFFIC investigations revealed that many circuses were using endangered animals of "questionable origin" – which meant that they were almost certainly obtained illegally and cruelly.

The worldwide trade in wild birds is brisk. Danish officials discovered a cargo of twenty-three African Grey parrots, seventeen rose-ringed parakeets and four Senegal parrots in a cargo ship going from Senegal to Moscow. Nearly three hundred birds, including crowned cranes, peacocks and Egyptian geese, were found during a random vehicle check on the border with France and Belgium.

The examples go on and on.

Bangkok's market

In the 1980s Thailand became known as the "wildlife supermarket of the world" – so much so that TRAFFIC staff launched an undercover investigation in the capital, Bangkok. There were no laws to stop the import and export of animals and investigators were horrified at what they found.

Thousands of live parrots, leopards, reptiles, orang-utans, monkeys and gibbons were sold in dreadful conditions; leopard-skin coats and tiger heads could be bought in the stores of Bangkok; markets sold rhino horn, tiger bone and monkeys' brains and millions of wild orchids were traded each year without any controls at all. TRAFFIC researchers also counted 112 shops in Bangkok selling tiger teeth and claws as necklaces and earrings. Forty-eight fresh bear paws were found in the refrigerator of a Bangkok restaurant.

This went on in a country that had signed an international treaty known as the Convention on International Trade in Endangered Species, CITES, of Wild Fauna and Flora, that controls commercial wildlife trade between the 117 countries that have signed it.

Action had to be taken.

WWF's answers

In April 1991, WWF set up an international campaign in which members wrote to the Thai government demanding effective laws to stop this trade. Many members wrote saying that they were going to operate a boycott on tourism which is one of Thailand's main sources of income. They pointed out the disgrace of having signed the CITES treaty and allowing this kind of trade to take place.

Within a year, Thailand's National Assembly passed new laws enforcing regulations and making trade in endangered wildlife illegal. Now, the government is working with TRAFFIC to strengthen trade controls.

WWF's long association with TRAFFIC is one of the most fruitful environmental partnerships ever developed. Like WWF, TRAFFIC works quietly behind the scenes, trying to persuade governments to change their wildlife laws when they are seen to be inadequate. And, if countries have not signed the CITES agreement, the WWF/TRAFFIC partnership helps to persuade them to do so.

Decline of the rhino

Of all the large endangered species in the world today, none is more at risk than the black rhinoceros which is hunted for its horn. In 1971, there were sixty-five thousand of these huge beasts in Africa. By the 1990s their numbers had fallen to a mere three thousand. This decline was so catastrophic that, despite the WWF and IUCN campaign to save the rhino launched in 1979, WWF continues to try to eliminate poaching.

An adult black rhino stands about 1.5 metres high, weighs a tonne or more and has two valuable horns. It also has dreadful eyesight, which makes the animal itself very nervous: any rapid movement nearby will excite it to attack and when angered it can reach speeds of fifty kilometres an hour. Its short-sightedness also creates another major problem: it is highly vulnerable to stealthy, rifle-carrying poachers.

The rhino spends most of its day gently ambling around dry scrubland feeding on twigs, leaves and any fruit it finds on shrubs and bushes. Like most animals in hot climates, it also enjoys a midday rest and a wallow in water. In that respect, it is a creature of habit and, therefore, easy for poachers to find.

Illegal trading

Rhino horn is a very tough, compacted growth of bristle and contains no nerves. It grows at the rate of six centimetres a year.

All trade in rhino horns is illegal. Yet, just like tiger bones, rhino horns are sold to traders who export them. More than half the illegal horn goes to Yemen, where it is carved, shaped and polished into handles for traditional daggers, called djambias. These are highly valued status symbols and, for at least eight hundred years, adolescent boys have received a djambia to mark their transition into manhood.

For generations, many people in the Far East have used rhino horn in medical treatments. They look back over a long history that goes as far back as 200 B.C. Today, it is used in laryngitis pills, in the treatment of fevers, headaches, depression and nosebleeds, as well as epilepsy and malaria.

Usually the medicine is sold over the counter, but some pharmacists buy the raw horn and prepare it themselves by slicing it into slithers and grinding it down into a fine powder. It is then added to other mixtures and dispensed to patients.

Western research into the medical benefits of rhino horn is largely inconclusive, although it is agreed that it does seem to reduce fever. It certainly has a strong psychological value – it tastes bitter, salty and sour and people believe it works, whether or not it does. Even though substitutes, such as water buffalo horn, are available, rhino horn is still considered best so the demand runs high; in some parts of the world it is three times as valuable as gold.

The smuggling chain

Belief in the medicinal quality of rhino horn goes much further than the traditional pharmacies of South-East Asia. The product is widely used by oriental communities throughout the world and has been found in cities as diverse as Los Angeles and Brussels. So how does it get to these places?

The poachers who go out and kill rhinos and other animals – facing the dangers of getting killed by the

The dull reality of the number of rhinos poached is apparent as their skulls are laid out side by side (opposite top). The magnificent horns (opposite bottom) look bizarre as they stand divorced from their natural owner. As well as the black rhino (above), there are four other species, all of which are endangered. The Javan rhino, from the Far East, is the rarest large mammal on earth, with numbers having been reduced from thousands to no more than one hundred.

Opposite top: To prevent rhinos from falling prey to poachers' bullets, some governments in Africa are moving them to private land where they can be better protected. They are darted, winched onto trucks and transported to safety. At the other end of their journey, the rhinos are held for several days in bomas – fenced off compounds – to calm them down before being released.

Opposite below: In order to render the rhino worthless to poachers, National Conservation officials remove each rhino's horn under sedation, resulting in horn fragments such as these.

Right: Having been ruthlessly stripped of its horn, the carcass of a rhino is found, abandoned and decaying; despite their efforts, the anti-poaching party is too late.

rhino or arrested by the authorities – are the first link in a long chain. For a single horn, they may receive up to US$200 which can be a significant sum of money, enough to keep a family in food for months. Dealers, sometimes working alone but more frequently in groups, then trade the horn on to overseas customers at hugely inflated prices because of rarity and risk. This is done using code words or signs to avoid detection by the authorities.

Once a price has been agreed, the horn is smuggled out of the country. A common way of doing this is to hide a single horn in a sack of flour, sugar or grain which is part of a large consignment destined to be shipped to North Africa or the Middle East. On many occasions, individuals slip a horn into their baggage or briefcase and hope they won't be searched by customs officials on their way.

Paying the price

Whichever method of transportation is used, the costs are high. From the start, there are people to be bribed, bills to be paid and, all the while, risk of detection by the authorities. Customs inspections can happen at any time and if TRAFFIC is on the trail, smugglers may be caught red-handed.

Once out of the country of origin (where rhino horn

will almost certainly be recognized for what it is), the smuggling process continues. By now, the horn may be repackaged and falsely marked, perhaps as cow or buffalo horn, and sent to its final destination, where it is received by an agent who takes a share of the profit and sells it on. For all these reasons, by the time the horn reaches a traditional pharmacy in the Far East, its price has shot up to sums the original poacher couldn't even dream about.

The dismal reality is that all efforts to save the black rhino have, so far, failed. WWF continues to pressure the governments of the four main dealing countries – Korea, Yemen, China and Taiwan – and trading in rhino horn has been banned internationally, yet still it goes on. The animals are still killed.

So what *is* the answer?

A desperate operation

One last desperate attempt has been adopted to stop the poachers. In Zimbabwe, where the black rhino population dropped from two thousand to five hundred in just one year, WWF pledged US$300,000 to a dehorning operation.

Under this scheme, groups of game wardens drive deep into the bush. With the aid of radios, a great deal of local knowledge and, if they are fortunate, a helicopter scout overhead, they pick up the trail of a rhino.

Then the chase is on. The rhino takes fright and the wardens must act quickly because they don't know how the beast will react. It could run away, or it may charge. One of the group takes aim...and fires.

But they are not firing bullets. They are operating a high-powered gun that shoots darts at a velocity high enough to pierce the rhino's tough hide to sedate the animal. Within four minutes the rhino is unconscious. Then the wardens move in on foot.

What happens next is gruesome to watch. A veterinary officer checks the animal and starts up a chainsaw. The rhino's horn is then deftly sliced from its face and the stump is filed down. The whole process takes just ten minutes.

This operation deprives rhinos of their principal weapon for defending themselves. A lion would

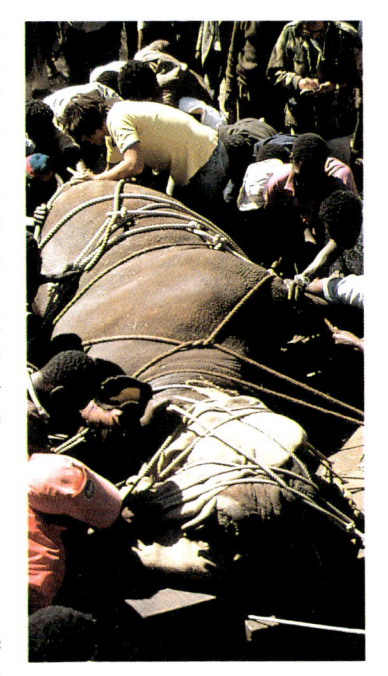

"...whereas the time scale of evolution is very long indeed, the time scale of extinction is often short and sharp."

Sir Peter Scott, 1981.

normally hesitate before threatening a rhino, especially if it had a calf. "But," remarked a WWF field officer, "a live dehorned rhino is better than a dead one. Poachers, not lions, are by far the bigger threat."

Breaking the habit

Veterinary officers believe that the rhinos suffer no pain after the operation and the horn will re-grow – which might create its own problems. If the dehorning operation is a success, it will have to become permanent. This would need long-term funding which is difficult to find.

To keep the rhinoceros from extinction, today's crucial challenge is to eliminate the demand for horn. People who have used it all their lives – and their parents and grandparents before them – have to be persuaded that a non-animal substitute is as good as or even better than the horn.

This is not necessarily an impossible task. WWF and other groups have campaigned, with some success, in Burundi, Hong Kong, Japan, Macao, Malaysia, the United Arab Emirates and Yemen, proving that the trade in rhino horn can be curtailed.

Holocaust at sea

WWF has long campaigned for the survival of another mammal being hunted to the point of extinction: the whale. A whale can leap high into the air, dive one thousand metres to the depths of the ocean, sing to its partner across great distances and travel at nearly fifty kilometres an hour. It is the biggest animal on earth. It has no enemies – except humans.

This same creature has been hunted almost to the point of extinction, so that humans could turn it into soap, candles, oil, margarine, cosmetics, drum skins, wax crayons and cooking fat. Whale oil was used to lubricate and power machinery, it lit street lamps, houses and even entire cities. Whale meat was canned and eaten by humans, as well as by their dogs and cats, and whale bone was used for stiffening collars and corsets. Every single segment of this giant, magnificent mammal was utilized.

Away from the harpoons, the blue whale has been known to live for more than one hundred years. It can weigh up to 150 tonnes, four times the weight of the largest known dinosaur.

*"From space, the planet is blue.
From space, the planet is the territory
Not of humans, but of the whale."*

Heathcote Williams, from "Whale Nation".

Whaling has gone on since the fourteenth century, but it was not until the nineteenth century that it became unsustainable. In 1864, a Norwegian, named Svend Foyn, invented an explosive harpoon that could be fired from a cannon. Aimed in front of the whale's flippers, the harpoon hit the lungs, heart or spinal area, and after a few seconds, exploded inside the animal. By the 1920s, factory ships the size of aircraft carriers were harpooning thirty thousand great whales in this way every year with deadly accuracy. The remaining whales simply could not breed enough numbers to regenerate the population as the slaughter was too complete.

Whales in decline

The whaling industry was so efficient and ruthless that species after species were decimated. First the blue whales – the biggest animal to have lived on earth, each one weighing as much as thirty elephants – then the fin whales and other, smaller species until the entire population was almost wiped out. By the 1990s, from the 250,000 blue whales that roamed the Southern Ocean of the Antarctic, there were just a thousand left.

In the 1930s, people began to realize that whale numbers were declining rapidly. Efforts to regulate hunting were made but with precious little impact and the slaughter continued unchecked. Then, in 1946, the International Whaling Commission, IWC, was founded to control whaling.

Once hunted using hand harpoons from wooden boats, whales are now killed with exploding harpoons before ending up in cans on supermarket shelves.

"... the struggle to save the whales has become a symbol of the wider battle to save the many thousands of animals and plants threatened with extinction by the greed, cruelty and short-sightedness of our own species."

Sir Peter Scott, 1986.

Cynical conservationists called the IWC the "International Whaling Club" because that is what it seemed to them to be – a club for whaling nations. It allowed whaling to continue with very few controls until, in 1972, a United Nations conference on the environment demanded a ten year moratorium on commercial whaling. Even then, it was another fourteen years before the IWC reluctantly agreed to stop the slaughter and re-think its policy.

Defying the ban

Over the years WWF has sponsored whale research projects all over the world. It sees no need for commercial whaling and it vigorously supports the establishment of a whale sanctuary in the Antarctic. There, these graceful, harmless creatures will be able to recover their depleted numbers away from the threat of harpoons and "scientific" whaling ships.

That threat is likely to return. In 1992, Iceland announced that it intended to resume whaling and there was nothing that the IWC or any other organization could do about it. Norway also wanted to kill whales for commercial profit. Japan has never given up whaling completely: it hunts whales for "scientific purposes". But WWF continues its campaign against the whaling countries.

In 1993, the IWC's annual conference was held in Japan, where the host nation and Norway continued to press for the resumption of commercial hunting of the small minke whale. Their requests were defeated, leading Norway to declare that it would ignore the ban and begin killing minkes anyway. WWF and other conservation organizations, such as Greenpeace, are deeply concerned that the hunting of one species will lead to other and rarer species, such as the blue whale, being killed as well.

"Operation Panda"

In 1979, the Chinese government invited Sir Peter Scott to advise it on how best to conserve the giant panda. Many had starved to death after huge mountain forests of bamboo – the panda's staple diet – had flowered and died instead of re-seeding. This strange phenomenon happens every forty to fifty years and it takes a whole year before the first shoots appear and re-grow. A full ten years may pass before stocks can recover sufficiently to support the one thousand pandas that are left in the wild.

Sir Peter Scott led a WWF delegation to Beijing and agreed to fund a project to establish a panda breeding station and research unit. The project, "Operation Panda", was set up in the Wolong Nature Reserve which covers some two thousand square kilometres in China. It was decided to raise money for it until 1981, WWF's twentieth birthday. There seemed no more suitable way of commemorating the anniversary than by doing something special for the animal that, in a way, helped to give birth to the organization.

Pandas in peril

Pandas are, by nature, very solitary animals so they are not frequent breeders. From the age of six, females can produce young, but in their fairly short life span of fourteen years, they rarely give birth to more than four or five cubs.

They are also fussy eaters. The eighty pandas in Wolong feed on just two species of bamboo, each animal consuming as much as twenty kilograms a day.

Wolong, like other panda habitats, is surrounded by

Pandas at WWF's research unit at Wolong in China. One is being artificially inseminated in an effort to increase the species' chance of survival, while another is being fitted with a radio transmitter so that zoologists can keep track of it. Through monitoring the pandas, researchers can work out why they do not like the most nutritious part of the bamboo plant and how the pandas endanger their own food supply by eating the fresh shoots of new plants.

A mountain gorilla and its young in Zaire. International trade in primates is fierce as many are used for research experiments. To educate people of the habits and nature of gorillas both in the wild and in parks, WWF sponsors public awareness schemes for farmers and local people and trains guides and rangers all over Africa.

agricultural land that is completely free of bamboo. Potatoes, corn and other crops are grown to help feed China's population of more than a billion people. When the supply of bamboo runs out, the animals are unable to move to new supplies because they are effectively trapped in by the farmed land. If the pandas cannot reach fresh bamboo, they gradually starve and die.

The pandas are also at risk because of poaching. Hundreds of snares have been found in the undergrowth of Wolong: snares set mainly for deer. But these vicious traps do not distinguish between one species and another. Consequently, many pandas have fallen victim, more by accident than design.

For all these reasons, pandas are extremely difficult to conserve. The Wolong project has proved to be disappointing, if not a failure, and the future of the animal remains uncertain.

However in 1993, WWF planned to finance the establishment of bamboo corridors between one reserve and another, in the hope that the pandas will move around and breed more freely. The corridors should also help ensure that the animals are never trapped without food supplies again.

"Save the jungle"

The lessons learned about the importance of habitat protection during WWF's "Operation Tiger" led to the organization adopting a major new strategy: saving the rainforests.

In 1975, WWF designated rainforests protected areas and launched an international appeal for money to "Save the jungle – save the world". Rainforest campaigns have continued ever since. Over US$2 million was raised for management schemes and educational courses. Trucks, supplied with posters and slide shows, toured the areas near the rainforests, showing the people why it was so vital that they keep the forest intact. Most of the early schemes were short-term and WWF gained valuable expertise and knowledge.

As well as setting up forest management schemes and training courses in Asia, Africa, Central America, Australia and some of the Pacific islands, WWF also

Above: The Stubbs Creek area in Nigeria is renowned for its wealth of endangered species such as the red cap mangabey. Conserving these areas is part of a project run by the Nigerian Conservation Foundation, an organization that has close links with WWF. Left: The main threat to the jaguar's survival is rainforest destruction. WWF manages the world's first jaguar sanctuary in Belize and runs a jaguar conservation project in Brazil.

warned the world about the growing dangers of uncontrolled logging – the felling of trees and the clearing of forests for commercial purposes.

The keepers of life

Rainforests play a significant part in balancing the global climate. They recycle rainfall and release moisture at a regular pace. They also draw in vast amounts of the gas carbon dioxide from the earth's atmosphere.

Rainforests house the most complex ecosystems, where unique plants and animals interact with each other in one habitat. They contain almost half of all known flora and fauna species. Their constant climate is ideal for plants which, when in bloom, attract thousands of birds, animals and insects. Yet that is only the beginning: scientists and biologists know that within these vast and dense forests more insects, fish and plants are yet to be discovered.

Essential oils, gums, latexes, resins, tannins, sweeteners, spices, bananas, avocados, Brazil nuts, cloves and cinnamon all come from the rainforests. At least a quarter of known medicines are from the forests and, of the three thousand plants identified by the US National Cancer Institute as having anti-cancer properties, 70% come from tropical rainforests.

Rainforests also provide cures for malaria, as well as increasingly successful treatments for epilepsy and blood cancer. It is possible that in due course a cure for AIDS will be found from forest sources, too.

Opposite top: Farmers clear forest land. This slash-and-burn policy destroys the rainforest and the land is exhausted in two to three years. The soil is then eroded by the rains (opposite below). WWF runs courses in countries like Cameroon to help the people find a sustainable way to make a living.

Scorched earth

Yet trees are cut down, burned and cleared for agriculture under a reckless slash-and-burn policy. Trees are cut for timber and as raw materials for other products – like paper – and most of the demand comes from the developed countries. The forests are abused to the point where thousands of different species that live in them are driven to extinction.

Tropical trees, like trees everywhere, draw minerals and nutrients from the soil so that they can flourish. But they retain the minerals from the soil, which then becomes barren. The soil is kept intact only by the tree canopy that deflects rainfall and heat.

The results of tree felling are disastrous. When the trees are felled, that canopy is instantly removed. The exposed soil rapidly turns to dust. It can rain up to two-and-a-half centimetres every day in the tropics so the dust is quickly washed away. Mud-slides and flooding, as in India and Bangladesh, can lead to a terrible loss of homes and human life. In 1991, more than seven thousand people drowned in the Philippines after flash floods poured down hillsides that had been denuded of rainforest.

But the world wants wood in great quantities and the tropics contain the finest hardwoods on earth. In the last ten years, vast areas of rainforest have been cleared to raise cattle for export to the American beefburger industry. To add to the pressure, more and more people living near the forests need agricultural land for crops

Above: $8 billion a year is no mean sum. This is the value of tropical timber exports to the developing countries; little wonder then, that logging is so difficult to keep in check.

There is much to be learned from the indigenous tribes of the rainforest, such as the Kayapo (above) and Surni Indians (right). For generations they have co-existed with their environment, never taking more than can be naturally replenished.

and their own modest cattle grazing, so they clear just a few more trees for a sparse patch of earth. After just two or three cropping seasons, the land becomes completely exhausted and barren.

Forcing the people out

More than 140 million people live in or around tropical rainforests. And, in the rainforests of Brazil, the life style of local tribes is under immediate threat as their land and villages are destroyed for dams, roads and timber felling.

"In this unexplored region [of the rainforest] there are a number of groups who have never been contacted by the white man," Chief Raoni of the Brazilian Kayapo Indians revealed. "When they are, they are in mortal danger from disease, the destruction of their land, even murder. Every year, the burning of the forest by the white settler gets closer and closer."

The terrible truth is that every minute of every day, another twenty-five hectares of the world's rainforest are destroyed as demand for wood and grazing land increases. Ninety tribes are thought to have disappeared in the Amazon forest of Brazil this century.

For hundreds of years, tribal people have inhabited the world's rainforests. In Malaysia, relics have been found from forty thousand years ago. One tribe still living in the Amazon is the Yanoama, also known as the Yanomani. Traditionally nomadic hunter-gatherers, they number about twenty thousand and are scattered in small communities throughout the Sierra Parima. They have no chiefs, believe in equality and regard selfishness as evil.

The Yanoama hunt animals and fish for protein and gather nuts and other fruits from the trees. Many of their communities, which rarely exceed fifty people, plant bananas, cassava, sweet potatoes, papaya, cane and gourds. They supplement their diet with the meat of game birds, armadillos, deer, capybara, monkeys and peccaries from the forest. Most of these creatures are tracked silently and killed by the Yanoamas' expert use of bows and arrows made from palm wood, silk grass and cane.

The coming together of two cultures: a Kayapo Indian from Brazil, adorned in traditional feather headdress and body decorations, but also wearing a modern wristwatch. Some conservationists believe traditional cultures are being ruined by Western influences, while others say that indigenous people are as entitled to have access to modern trends as anyone else.

Invasion

In the 1950s, the Yanoama's territory was invaded, first by Christian missionaries and then by mineral and land developers. That invasion has never stopped.

While the missionaries were looking for converts, the developers were seeking rights to the enormous wealth of manganese, gold, copper, bauxite and iron ore deposits to be found in the Amazon. The loggers were not far behind them. By the 1970s, roads were being built and mines sunk. Trees were being felled and land cleared so that ranchers could set up lucrative businesses supplying meat to the world's ever-growing appetite for fast food. No one cared about the indigenous tribes who lived on the land.

WWF funds conservation education schemes in the Korup National Park in Cameroon, Africa. The schemes give information and knowledge to the people of the country so that they can manage the wealth of the rainforests themselves.

The intruders brought with them machinery for digging, explosives for blasting and chain-saws for tree felling. They also brought influenza, chickenpox, whooping cough and other ailments. These were common enough illnesses in the industrialized, wealthy world, but quite unknown among the tribespeople.

The result was devastating. Entire villages were all but wiped out as diseases reached epidemic proportions. In some communities as many as nine out of ten people died.

"WWF has changed in the three decades of its existence [1961-1991] from an organisation concerned primarily about species, to one striving to stop the destruction of the world's natural resources."

Mark Carwardine, from "The WWF Environment Handbook".

New opportunities

If exposure to missionaries, developers, ranchers and loggers brought sickness and death, it also provided new ideas and opportunities. Steel tools and cooking pots, metal arrow points, drills, scissors and fish hooks all became commonplace. Tribespeople were exposed to electrical goods and what they saw, some not unnaturally wanted for themselves.

Until this time the Yanoama were entirely self-sufficient. They grew or hunted what they needed for food and they bartered other goods with each other. But as the opening of roads, mines and ranches gathered pace, some indigenous people took jobs and became reliant on the newcomers. For the first time in thousands of years, the Yanoama were no longer independent.

While some environmentalists bemoaned the fact that a number of tribes were abandoning their traditional lifestyles, others pointed out that they had every right to be part of the modern world. WWF's belief is that all people must be given unfettered access to information so that they can make choices from a position of strength and understanding.

This is why WWF provides education and practical help to communities living in and around the forests. In Cameroon, in West Africa, for example, it gives technical assistance to the managers of the Korup National Park. This is one of the most biologically diverse forests containing the largest number of plant species of any rainforest in Africa. Without protection it would disappear by the year 2010.

WWF helps to finance the park and has created buffer zones around it. These are twice the size of the park, and hunting, fishing and forestry can be carried out there without posing a threat to the park itself.

Changing direction

Over time, WWF became increasingly aware of the importance of the delicate balance between humans, wildlife and the environment. So, in 1980 it formally broadened its outlook and changed its direction. Expanding its task from protecting wildlife and habitats, WWF looked harder at the wider aspects of life on earth. The outcome of this was the creation of the World Conservation Strategy.

This declared that humanity had no future unless nature and the world's natural resources were conserved. Conservation, it said, could not be achieved

In response to the WWF "Guardian of the Rainforest" campaign, Anita Roddick, of the Body Shop, pledged to help raise funds, saving several thousand hectares of rainforest.

Below: Doctors working on medicines derived from wild plants at Yaounde University in Cameroon. Products developed in this way bring the country that is home to the rainforest increased wealth.

Seedlings of success...the contrast of cultivated crops among the trees of the rainforest; the agroforestry campaign in Sumatra pictured here shows that theory can be put into effective practice.

unless plans to develop the world would also help relieve the poverty and misery of countless millions of people. The World Conservation Strategy spoke for the first time about "sustainable development" – a concept that has been central to WWF's thinking ever since.

Sustainable development means that only what nature can replenish is used by humankind; that more than can be re-generated is not taken; that people share resources and ideas with each other and care for the earth at the same time. It means adopting lifestyles and development plans that work within nature's limits.

Agroforestry

One such scheme introduced by WWF, in support of "sustainable development", was the successful technique of agroforestry. This is a system of planting trees and farm crops side by side: the tree roots grow deep into the ground, bind the soil and act as a nutrient pump for the crops that then flourish.

There are also WWF's agricultural training courses for local farmers. They learn how to plant and care for crops that are suitable for the soil and that will feed the people as well as provide them with an income. This leads to better health in local villages – and with health and good feeding comes the strength to work.

There are similar success stories in other parts of the world – in Indonesia, for example, in China, Central America, Brazil, Chile and Peru. WWF's worldwide forest conservation scheme for trees and people in the 1990s covers twelve million hectares in some thirty countries. Its target is to see one hundred million hectares of tropical rainforest protected by the end of the twentieth century.

Top: WWF has encouraged schemes whereby local people make use of the products of the forest, as above in the Korup National Park, without hunting or poaching. Above: Farm workers harvest angiroba, a valuable medicinal oil.

A seventh of the world's land surface is covered by desert. Though they can take millions of years to form, once established they can expand rapidly. Deforestation is a major factor contributing to the extensive growth of desert areas.

Governments, forestry commissions, land owners, local politicians and ordinary people have all become involved in trying to achieve this goal. WWF and other conservation groups constantly strive to raise people's awareness.

There are some signs that governments that manage tropical forests are now setting targets of their own. More and more are coming to understand the importance of harvesting trees and planting at the same time, thereby sustaining the environment.

The warnings sounded by WWF – ever more urgent with each year that passes – are slowly but surely being heeded. Even so, there is a long way to go before effective targets are reached. In Africa, only one hectare of rainforest is planted for every seventy cut down – a clear example of use that cannot be sustained. Worldwide, the ratio is a depressing one to ten.

The World Bank

Some people in industrialized countries feel that the governments of the countries involved should prevent their forests being cut down for the good of the planet. However, the poorer countries, where most of the forests exist, need money and that sometimes has to be their only consideration.

Many developing countries import goods such as food, oil and machinery so that their people can survive. However, these governments often cannot afford to pay for these imports and when debts are not paid, interest is added to the original cost. The government may then have to borrow money to pay the interest.

Over the years, many countries have become crippled by debt and owe more in interest than the original amount borrowed. They may then turn to the World Bank.

The World Bank was created in 1945 to help raise the standard of living in developing countries. It enables money supplied by the industrialized countries to be spent in the poorer countries. Most of the funds are used for major projects such as dams, roads or power stations – projects that are too expensive for a small country to take on by itself.

Working harder, becoming poorer

Strict conditions are laid down before any loan is made by the World Bank. These might include forcing the country to increase food or energy prices to raise more money to help pay off the debt.

But when prices go up and services are cut back, the people have to work much harder and they become poorer. Their governments tell them to fell more trees, produce more coffee, copper, bananas or pineapples for the world market. But if several countries do this at the same time (as has frequently happened) a glut can occur. Too much of one product leads to prices tumbling and when that happens, standards of living fall and countries have to start borrowing again.

So people who fell rainforests often have no choice. Rich countries want timber and timber may have

Famine, drought and disease are nothing new to Africa and scenes of starvation are still common. WWF supports specific projects where, under controlled management, the local communities are able to use certain wildlife for a food source. In Botswana, for example, the spring hare yields three million kilograms of meat per year. This is a controversial scheme, so where WWF is involved it is subject to strict conditions.

Mexico City, as well as being one of the highest capital cities in the world, also has the dubious distinction of being among the most polluted. Much of the air pollution is caused by vehicle exhaust fumes.

been part of the loan conditions. The very governments that protest at forest destruction are sometimes the ones that have done deals to get hold of the timber in the first place.

Global warming

One of the most urgent environmental problems related to deforestation is global warming or the "greenhouse effect". The temperature of the planet will rise by between 1.5°C and 4.5°C by the middle of the next century.

WWF's concern about global warming focuses on forests. Trees are the earth's great storehouses of carbon dioxide which is the gas now recognized as being the main cause of global warming. This gas is released naturally into the earth's atmosphere by events like volcanic eruptions, but it is the human activities, such as the burning of coal, gas and oil that is exaggerating the effect.

In the process of growth, trees absorb carbon dioxide in vast quantities. When the trees are destroyed by

Industrial pollution, exhaust fumes and the CFCs generated from refrigerators all add to the level of nitrogen oxide in the earth's atmosphere. This, and other gases, then reacts with sunlight and water to create "acid rain". Stripping the trees here in Poland, acid rain falls all over the planet as it is carried along by the wind. Liming, or spraying ground-up limestone, is one of Sweden's short-term measures to neutralize the acidity in its lakes and rivers.

> *"If CFC emissions were reduced to zero today, the chemical reactions that are depleting the ozone layer would continue for at least a century."*
>
> Mark Carwardine, from "The WWF Environment Handbook".

burning, the carbon dioxide they have stored is released back into the atmosphere.

When this happens, it joins other gases and together they encircle and envelop the earth like a cocoon, forming a "shell" of gas around the world. This shell allows the rays from the sun to reach the earth, but it traps the heat in, just as a greenhouse does – which is why it is known as the "greenhouse effect". The result of the increase in these gases is that the earth's temperature is rising dangerously.

The main implication of this global warming is the melting of the polar ice-caps. This would then lead to a rise in the world's sea levels, which could result in the catastrophic flooding and wiping out of entire habitats and countries.

Trees cover a third of the world's land surface, in every climate from the northern reaches of Canada, Asia and Europe to the desolate wastes of Latin America. Temperate forests – those that thrive in moderate climates away from the tropics – have gone unnoticed for years but they too are now at risk.

WWF's most important forestry priorities are to see deforestation stopped by the year 2000 and to persuade the international timber trade to operate immediate short-term policies of "sustainable use". In 1993 the short-term date was set for 1995. A forestry official explained why they set such an optimistic time-scale, "If we weren't pushing for 1995, nothing would be happening at all".

The delicate balance

Another crucial element in the delicate, natural balance of the planet is wetlands.

Swamps, marshes, shallow seas, bogs, land seasonally flooded by rivers and lakes, estuaries and tidal flats – all these are wetlands. They are where earth and water meet and they exist everywhere from the tropics to frozen wastes.

Wetlands are not wastelands. They are alive and full of varied wildlife. The rapid plant growth in wetlands is a result of the high levels of mineral accumulation that come from surrounding regions. They vary incredibly in size. Ghadira, in Malta, covers a mere six hectares, while the Canadian Arctic bays extend to ten million hectares. Big or small, north or south, their function is much the same: they provide humans with fuel, food, recreation and employment, they support wildlife that would otherwise become extinct and they play a vital part in flood control.

A typical example of a tropical wetland is a mangrove swamp. Mangroves are inter-tidal forests that support an astonishing range of wildlife. Some mangroves are strategically planted between land and sea to protect nearby communities from violent storms and powerful sea waves. Mangrove roots spread beneath the water to trap sediment and to prevent it being washed out to sea; the result is an area of stillness and calm where fish can breed, birds take refuge and local people can earn a living from occupations such as bee keeping.

Otters, lynx, capercaillies, black storks, black grouse and rare eagle owls inhabit the Sumava Biosphere Reserve in the Czech Republic. The reserve is one of the most valuable natural areas in central Europe, where some species of tree and the Moorland clouded yellow butterfly have survived since the Ice Age, ten thousand years ago. WWF is assisting the Czech government in its conservation plans for the Sumava reserve.

Top soil dramatically being washed away into the sea...the mangrove that once grew on the shore here in Haiti has been felled taking the stability of the land with it. When the rains come, the soil turns to mud and is washed away into the sea.

A world away from the mangroves is the Wadden Sea. The Wadden Sea is the part of the North Sea that stretches along the coasts of the Netherlands, Germany and Denmark. It is marshy, salty and sandy. The water is shallow and the tidal mudflats – the sea bed that becomes exposed when the tide is out – play host to a wonderful range of seabirds, waders and seals. It supports no less than 80% of the North Sea's plaice, half the sole and nearly all the herring. If wetlands are destroyed, many existing plants and animal species will simply die out.

The Kafue Flats in Zambia, where WWF operates a large range of environmental projects, are home to the sea eagle and the boomslang snake. This vast floodplain of grassland, hot springs, swamp and woodlands

Wetlands, such as the Kafue Flats in Zambia, pictured here, are home to a variety of waterbirds and waders, as well as semi-aquatic reptiles and mammals, from otters and mink to crocodiles, watersnake and hippopotamuses in the warmer wetlands.

straddles the River Kafue which floods every December to reach its peak in May; then the waters subside until they reach their lowest ebb in November.

The Kafue Flats are one of the ten most notable bird sanctuaries in the world, and two major wildlife reserves have also been established there.

Drowning wetlands...

These three examples illustrate how different wetlands can be. Yet hundreds are in trouble – which is why WWF is involved in practical schemes and scientific research throughout the world.

The rising sea levels caused by global warming are having their effect. Shallow wetlands are becoming swamped, delicate plantlife drowns and the wildlife perishes or moves away. It is the same with swamps: when the water level rises, some species of mangrove will become completely submerged and the trees will drown. If that happens, the result will be catastrophic.

If this is not enough, wetlands the world over have to endure pollution in all its forms – from the air, from metals in the ground or from oil spillages at sea. Another growing problem is the fact that human beings are using too much water while at the same time draining many wetlands for agricultural use such as prawn farming.

...and parched trees

Countless millions of litres of water are stored in natural reservoirs underground. Trees and plants draw their supplies from this source, the water table.

But the more water is taken for agriculture, new housing, industrial and tourist developments as well as for everyday needs, the more the water table drops – sometimes to the extent that trees and plants can no longer reach it and are starved of their supplies. The result is that they wither and die.

There is some hope that this damaging chain of events can be slowed down and the answer partly lies in an international wetlands protection treaty agreed in the Iranian town of Ramsar in 1971. The Ramsar Convention is the world's oldest global conservation treaty and is signed by seventy-four countries. There are now more than six hundred wetland sites on Ramsar's list and were it not for the Convention, many of them would have disappeared long ago.

But the Ramsar Convention will only be as effective as its weakest members want it to be. If the world's threatened wetlands are to stand a chance of flourishing, more countries have to sign up and deal with the problem seriously – without delay.

At a meeting in Switzerland in 1990 Ramsar accepted a WWF proposal to establish a Wetlands Conservation Fund to finance projects in developing countries. Chile, Congo, Kenya, Mauritania and Vietnam have already been helped and the future for their wetlands is more hopeful than it was.

In 1991, mangrove areas were being destroyed at a rate of five hundred thousand hectares a year in Asia alone. The destruction of mangroves leads to the breakdown of other habitats, such as coral reefs. Reefs are choked by silt which was once trapped by mangroves; this quickly destroys these rich marine habitats.

Identifying areas

WWF has identified the Philippines – a country that comprises more than seven thousand islands in the Pacific Ocean – as possessing some of Asia's most threatened wetlands. The danger comes through pollution, from exhaustion due to over-use and because many sites are drained and converted to land production. Between 70%-90% of the Philippines' coastal wetlands have been destroyed or degraded in just thirty years. In the 1990s, only thirty thousand hectares of mangroves remain, compared to 450,000 hectares in the late 1960s.

Much of the solution is down to government responsibility and to Ramsar countries applying pressure. But it is also where WWF and other conservation organizations bring all their expertise to bear. They do this by advising governments, preparing wetland conservation and management plans, training people to become wetland rangers and keepers, and making people aware of the great importance of wetlands to their own lives.

In the Philippines, WWF has made possible the planting of over seventy thousand mangrove seedlings, with thousands more under way.

The Mai Po marshes and ponds of Hong Kong are among the most important wetland sites in the world – but despite that accolade, they are not safe. Parts of the marshes are being reclaimed for badly-needed housing projects. Hong Kong has a population of six million who live 5,500 to the square kilometre. By comparison, people in Hungary live 113 to the square kilometre, in the United Kingdom the figure is 236 and in the United States it is 26.

> "Mankind's compulsion [is] to take on and defeat the natural world. The explorer has always been followed by the conqueror...But whereas the explorer comes to marvel, the conqueror comes to despoil. Antarctica has been explored.
> Now the conquerors are gathering."
>
> *From "Antarctica", a Greenpeace publication.*

Antarctica – the last wilderness

Antarctica is often described as the most beautiful place in the world. Conservationists call it the last wilderness on earth – a place so cold, so frozen, so windy and so inhospitable that no human being can live there permanently. Like the wetlands, it, too, is under threat and needs to be protected by countries consenting to preserve it.

Temperatures can fall to -80°C and they never rise above -35°C around the South Pole. Even so, more than two hundred species of lichen as well as mosses, fungi and the occasional flowering plant survive. Peat beds three metres thick have been discovered on this continent which is home to one hundred million birds.

Unlike the Arctic, which is a vast ice-pack floating on

A group of Adelie penguins takes the sun at the water's edge, in Antarctica. A hundred million birds visit or live in this vast natural wilderness. In 1991, the future of Antarctica remaining untouched was secured for fifty-five years. Research in Antarctica's unspoiled environment enables scientists to assess global damage and what the future holds for the earth and our lifestyles.

the sea, Antarctica is a land mass. It has, therefore, attracted scientists, mineralogists and geologists keen to discover what wealth lies beneath the frozen land.

They suspect that untold quantities of oil, silver, gold, copper and other precious commodities are there, ready to be exploited. It takes little effort to imagine the ecological disaster that would happen if the sinking of oil wells and the mining of minerals were allowed in Antarctica. That is what a number of countries want to happen.

Digging for gold

In 1988, an international treaty was agreed that would have allowed prospecting for minerals to take place. Conservationists immediately set to work persuading

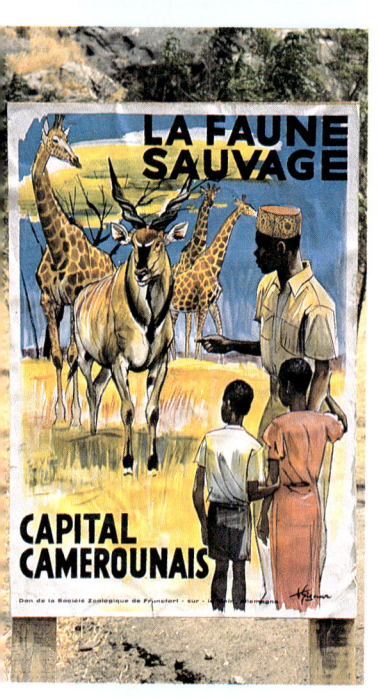

As part of the effort to heighten awareness, a poster promoting the need to protect the wildlife is donated to the WAZA National Park, in Cameroon, by the Frankfurt zoological society.

the world of the folly of what it was doing. The French marine scientist and environmentalist, Jacques Cousteau, and the first explorer to walk to both the North and South Poles, Robert Swan, linked with WWF and Greenpeace in a global campaign to have the treaty scrapped. What they wanted in its place was the Antarctic to be designated a World Park, where mining would be illegal.

Jacques Cousteau led such a strong campaign that two million people (three quarters of them in France) signed his petition against the treaty. The French government soon announced that it would agree to the wishes of the public. WWF and Greenpeace organized another million signatures in the United Kingdom alone. The Australian government bowed to pressure. So did Japan, the United Kingdom, the United States and each of the remaining thirty-four countries that had drawn up the original treaty.

The result was that a new agreement came into force in 1991. It banned all prospecting, oil drilling and mining in the Antarctic for at least fifty-five years and it completely replaced the original treaty which, thanks to ordinary people, never saw the light of day. Antarctica had been saved from exploitation, at least for half a century.

Looking back and looking forward

By the time WWF reached its twenty-fifth anniversary in 1986, it had invested US$110 million in more than four thousand projects in 130 countries.

While the image of any organization is important, so, too, is its policy. As the 1990s approached, WWF decided to look back on what it had achieved, and what it had not, and to look ahead to new directions for a new century.

An independent report concluded that 73% of WWF's projects had been successful, at least in the short term. No one could deny that such a record was anything other than impressive. Even so, other projects had not had the hoped-for results. These included the panda breeding station in China and the campaign to save the rhino.

The report's findings underlined the difficult task

faced by conservationists the world over. Commercial ventures and human greed damage or destroy land, wildlife and habitats continuously. But were it not for WWF, Greenpeace, Friends of the Earth, the World Conservation Union and other groups across the globe, the carnage would be much worse. The polar bear would now be a picture in a book. The whale would be an unseen rarity. Hundreds of tropical and temperate forests would be stumps in the ground and the oceans and seas would be dumping sites for every kind of toxic waste imaginable.

Conservation projects such as saving the forests, wetlands or the rhino operation naturally cost a great deal of money.

More than half of WWF's worldwide income is from donations sent by individual members of the organization – the most important people in the world to any charity.

In 1971, the president of WWF International, Prince Bernhard of the Netherlands, developed an interesting scheme that was to prove a long-lasting success. He

High school students in Damarland, Namibia, visit a natural spring where elephants, rhinos and other animals come to drink. Much can be learned about animals and their habits simply by surveying and analyzing their feeding and watering grounds.

invited one thousand people around the world each to contribute US$10,000 for a US$10 million trust fund, the income from which would cover WWF International's administration costs. The fund was named "The 1001 Club: A Nature Trust" (the extra one being Prince Bernhard himself). It took two and a half years before the final donor was signed up and the trust has fulfilled its task ever since.

The interest from the fund, together with profits from royalties and trading, has ensured that WWF has been able to keep an important pledge: that the money donated by the public to WWF International for conservation is spent on conservation. Not a cent, a franc, a peseta, a zloty or a crown is spent on WWF headquarters' administration.

To become a member of the 1001Club today, donors must pay a contribution of at least US$25,000. There is even a waiting list.

Several governments make grants to various WWF overseas schemes and business organizations make donations that are often tied up with sponsorship. These deals frequently have the added bonus of publicity which makes the public more aware of WWF and the work it is doing.

"Mission for the 1990s"

When WWF came to work out the policy that would guide its future strategies and campaigns all these factors, and new ones besides, had to be taken on board.

The world has changed a great deal during the lifetime of WWF. The human population has almost doubled. Deserts have spread and water reserves have shrunk. Pollution has pervaded rivers, seas, land and the atmosphere. Poverty has increased and the technological gulf between the rich countries, now called "the North", and the poor countries, "the South", has widened.

The policy expressed, in one sentence, the very reason for WWF's existence: "To stop, and eventually reverse, the accelerating degradation of our planet's natural environment, and to help build a future in which humans live in harmony with nature."

To back the policy, or "Mission for the 1990s", WWF announced plans to spend US$150 million over five years on field projects in Africa, Asia and South America, and a further US$120 million on education and conservation, lobbying governments and making people more aware than ever that conservation matters. As if to hammer home the urgency of the Mission, WWF, together with the World Conservation Union and the United Nations Environment Programme (UNEP), published an important strategy document in 1991. "Caring for the Earth" set out 132 practical actions for governments, businesses, organizations, groups and individuals to implement. Then, one of the most important environmental conferences the world has ever seen took place: the "Earth Summit".

The Earth Summit

In the Brazilian city of Rio de Janeiro, in June 1992, the United Nations Conference on Environment and Development, the "Earth Summit" was held.

It was the world's largest international conference and dealt with the global environment. Not just the air and the water, but basic human indignities, such as poor countries being in debt to rich ones, individual poverty, famine, illness and the absence of birth control. This was a conference that, for the first time, linked the environment to the way in which humans were developing the world.

For eighteen months before the conference, WWF had been arguing in meetings with governments and with the United Nations itself for conventions on international debt, environmentally sound trade and taxes on energy consumption. It also called for the North to share its technological knowledge with the South. And WWF wanted firm agreements to conserve the planet's natural resources and to protect the variety of nature in the world.

Politicians and heads of state from 160 countries went to the conference to see and be seen. So did environmental organizations that had lobbied, argued and fought for vital issues to be raised. They wanted more than just talk. They wanted action.

This page and opposite: When necessary, WWF backs up its research work by public demonstration, in its effort to protect wildlife and lessen pollution.

Right: WWF takes to the skies to make its presence known at the Earth Summit in Brazil, in June 1992. Here, the future of the natural world, and our existence in it, was debated by 160 countries.

Opposite top: A family of orang-utans come down to the feeding platform in the WWF-sponsored Bohorok visitor unit in the Gunung Leuser National Park, Indonesia.
Opposite middle and bottom: Protective cages are placed over green turtle eggs in a hatchery in Pakistan; while an exhausted green turtle, having laid its eggs, is protected on its journey back to sea.

Getting somewhere?

In the end, two important treaties were signed at the Earth Summit – one to regulate global warming, the other to protect our biological diversity. Biological diversity is the variety of species found in the rainforests, wetlands, deserts and other unique habitats in the world. The treaty aimed to conserve those areas and, therefore, the undiscovered species in them. It also aimed to enable those developing countries with the habitats in them, particularly the rainforests, to share in the wealth that the scientific discoveries can generate. To the dismay of many delegates, the United States was the only industrialized country that refused to sign the biodiversity treaty.

The American government had come under incredible pressure from its own biotechnology industry – a section of business so big, so varied and so powerful that its demands (and its financial strength) seemed to be impossible to ignore.

Biotechnology touches on almost every walk of life including pharmaceuticals, food, agriculture, genetic engineering, paints, even washing powders and clothes. The industry did not like the treaty because it did not want to share the vast profits that could be generated from scientific discoveries. So the then president, George Bush, refused to sign the treaty.

It took a year, a new president in the White House and a change in government policy before America agreed to sign.

North and South, rich and poor

Unless the governments of the North change their attitudes and co-operate with the poorer countries of the South, very little progress will be made. The issues of poverty, bad housing, illness, hunger and other social deprivations are bound up with global warming and the well-being of nature. People are as much a part of nature as are any other creatures or plants – although with one important difference. People dominate nature.

In that respect, humanity has the whole world in its hands. When we care for ourselves, we care for our planet. This is just another reason why conservation organizations and pressure groups are so important: to bring pressure to bear on governments, to remind them of their environmental responsibilities and to keep them to their promises.

Looking ahead: the continuing struggle

WWF is one of many environmental organizations that fight to safeguard the world's rich storehouse of biological diversity. Human beings share the planet with some 1,400,000 known species in the major animal and plant groups, as well as the estimated 8,500,000 undiscovered species, up to 90% of which live in tropical forests.

But ozone layer depletion, acid rain, emissions of greenhouse gases, the rise in sea levels, soil erosion and human activities all take a heavy toll. If climate change accelerates, matters may get far worse than they are now.

Feeding Capybara in Brazil - WWF tackles the problems of endangered species and threatened habitats by finding positive solutions and raising money to get those schemes implemented.

"No government or organization, no matter how well its intention may be, can tackle the root of the [environmental] problem without the awareness and participation of everyone in society. That is why the efforts of WWF are so important and should be supported wholeheartedly by all of us."

His Holiness the Dalai Lama, 1984.

The roots of the crisis facing nature lie in the growing human population, the greedy consumption of natural resources and the materialistic consumer lifestyle enjoyed by people in industrialized countries. Nearly 40% of the productivity of plants, algae and bacteria are consumed, diverted or destroyed by the North.

There are 5.3 billion people in the world today. Some forecasters say that within sixty years numbers will more than double to a staggering twelve billion. So sustainability – not taking more of a natural resource than is put back – is at the heart of our future.

Sharing to survive

Sustainability, however, goes further than just keeping within limits.

The benefits gained from the world's natural resources must be shared evenly among peoples and nations. Everyone must have access to education and information which, in some parts of the world where those basics are denied, raises human rights issues.

One of WWF's challenges is to make that point clear to governments and influential people everywhere. Another is to help people understand what must be done if our natural world is to thrive. Reliable information must be readily available so that people can make informed choices. This is a central theme of WWF's work in its thousands of worldwide projects and its education schemes.

WWF has come a long way since its founding in 1961. From its modest beginnings, it has grown into a substantial organization that has made the environment a matter of world concern. It is the only international environmental organization to raise money, lobby governments, conduct research and set up its own schemes and projects on a worldwide basis. Now, decision-makers and political leaders listen to what WWF has to say. Scientists, biologists and other experts turn to the organization for advice.

As the world approaches a new century, complex environmental challenges will appear. Advanced solutions will need to be found and WWF will continue to be at the forefront, playing an active and significant role.

Important dates

1948	The International Union for the Conservation of Nature and Natural Resources (IUCN) is established.
1961	The IUCN moves its headquarters to Morges, Switzerland. World Wildlife Fund (WWF) is created in collaboration with IUCN. May: The "Morges Manifesto", a document highlighting the need for such a fund, is signed by sixteen leading ecologists. Prince Bernhard of the Netherlands is appointed president of World Worldlife Fund International. Sept 11: WWF officially comes into existence and is registered as a charity in Zurich, Switzerland.
1971	Prince Bernhard of the Netherlands launches "The 1001: A Nature Trust", an exclusive club formed in order to generate donations for WWF and the IUCN.
1972	Oct: WWF launches "Operation Tiger", which runs parallel with the Indian government's "Project Tiger" – a plan to set up nine national parks as tiger reserves.
1973	The Convention on International Trade in Endangered Species of Wild Fauna and Flora (CITES), an international wildlife organization, is established in an attempt to control and stop international trading of endangered plants and animals and products derived from them. The Polar Bear Agreement is signed by the five arctic nations to protect the polar bear and its habitat.
1975	The CITES treaty comes into force. The Ramsar Convention on Wetlands of International Importance comes into force to protect wetlands and conserve them and the habitat they provide for many flora and fauna species. WWF pioneers its first tropical rainforest campaign.
1976	The organization, Trade Records Analysis of Flora and Fauna in Commerce (TRAFFIC), is launched to ensure the CITES agreement is then enforced. This involves monitoring international trade in and the smuggling of endangered and protected animal and plant wildlife.
1979	Sir Peter Scott is invited to China to discuss the future of the giant panda. WWF launches a fund to establish the Wolong Nature Reserve in China, for the protection of pandas.
1980	WWF, IUCN and United Nations Environmental Programme (UNEP) launch the "World Conservation Strategy", to promote the concept of living within the limits of the natural environment.
1986	A ban on whaling imposed by the International Whaling Commission (IWC) comes into effect. WWF commemorates its silver jubilee, (twenty-five-years), at Assisi, Italy. World Wildlife Fund International adopts the new name of World Wide Fund For Nature (WWF), except in Canada and the United States of America where the name remains the same.
1987	The IUCN becomes the World Conservation Union.

1990   WWF and TRAFFIC research leads to the international banning of trade in ivory products.
WWF announces its "Mission for the 1990s".

1991   WWF, the World Conservation Union and UNEP launch "Caring for the Earth", a strategy for sustainable living in sixty countries.
Oct 4: An international agreement bans prospecting, oil drilling and mining in Antarctica for fifty-five years.

1992   June: The Earth Summit, or the United Nations Conference on Environment and Development (UNCED), is held in Rio de Janeiro, Brazil. The conference is called to consider important conservation issues world wide.
Iceland and Norway announce their intention to resume commercial whaling.

1993   May: IWC holds a conference in Japan at which the ban on whaling is kept intact. Norway threatens to start whaling commercially once again.

Further Information

If you would like further information about the work of WWF, or you would like to become a member, contact the main office in your country.

WWF – Australia
Level 10
8-12 Bridge Street
GPO Box 528
Sydney, NSW 2001
Phone 02 247 6300

WWF – Canada
90 Eglinton Avenue E.
Suite 504
Toronto
Ontario, M4P 2Z7
Phone 416 489 8800

WWF – International
World Conservation Centre
Avenue du Mont-Blanc
1196 Gland
SWITZERLAND
Phone 41 (22) 364 91 11

WWF – New Zealand
PO Box 6237
Wellington
Phone 04 499 2930

WWF – South Africa
PO Box 456
Stellenbosch
7600
Phone 2231 72801

WWF – United Kingdom
Panda House
Weyside Park
Godalming
Surrey, GU7 1XR
Phone 0483 426444

WWF – United States
1250 24th Street NW
Washington D.C.
20037-1175
Phone 202 293 4800

Glossary

Acid rain: Created when gases from smoke and exhaust fumes are released in large quantities into the atmosphere. The gases mix with water forming diluted acid, which falls as acid rain, eroding buildings and destroying wildlife.

CFCs: Chlorofluorocarbons (CFCs) are chemicals which are used in a variety of products, including refrigerators. When CFCs are released into the air, the chlorine in CFC chemicals breaks down the *ozone layer*. CFCs also contribute to the "greenhouse gases", which retain heat, adding to the danger of *global warming*.

Conservation: The protection, preservation and management of the earth, its environment and its natural resources.

Dodo: A flightless bird that lived on the island of Mauritius, in the Indian Ocean. Easily hunted by humans and other animals, it became extinct in the late seventeenth century.

Ecosystem: A mini-society of living creatures and plants that interact with one another in their particular *habitat*. Any changes made to this *habitat* affect its creatures and plants, which in turn can affect the existence of related ecosystems.

Extinction: The gradual reduction in the number of a particular animal or plant species to the point where it dies out and ceases to exist.

Fauna: All animal life.

Flora: All plant life.

Fossil fuel: Made from the fossilized remains of plants that existed millions of years ago, fossil fuels come from the ground (e.g. coal, oil or gas) and contain chemical elements including carbon and nitrogen. The chemicals are released into the atmosphere when the fuels are burned, contributing to the "greenhouse effect".

Geologist: A person who studies the earth, looking at its origin and history; considering the earth's structure and processes that go on within this structure.

Global warming: Also known as the "greenhouse effect". A build-up of gases, in particular carbon dioxide and *CFCs*, prevents the loss of heat from the earth's atmosphere, making the planet's temperature rise.

Glut: A situation where there is so much of one product that the market is flooded and the product's value falls substantially.

Habitat: The natural environment of a plant, animal or human.

Indigenous: When a person, animal or plant is born in, or is natural to, a country or particular *habitat*.

Mangrove: A tropical tree or shrub, which grows in a dense grove or forest, found in swamp regions and where freshwater areas meet the sea. Mangroves often act as a barrier between the two zones and have special root systems which cut down the movement of water around them. This protects the shore from erosion and inland areas from stormy seas. Mangroves are one of the few land plants that have adapted to living in both salt and fresh water.

Mineralogist: Someone who studies minerals (a natural, inorganic material such as coal) looking at the chemical make-up and structure of the mineral.

Moratorium: The legal delay of an act or policy. While it may prevent action for a certain amount of time (e.g. put a stop to commercial whaling), it is not a permanent ban.

Nutrient: A substance that provides nourishment to plants, animals or humans.

Ornithologist: A person who studies birds, their habits and their interaction with the environment.

Ozone layer: A fragile layer, twenty to fifty kilometres above the earth's surface, made from an oxygen-related gas called ozone. It creates a protective layer, filtering ultraviolet rays from the sun before they reach the earth.

Sediment: Particles of matter, often earth, that are carried by water and which settle on the bed of a river or other watercourses. In time, sediment builds up, sometimes to the extent that rivers and streams overflow.

Soil erosion: This happens when land is deprived of necessary *nutrients* or is over grazed by animals. Usual plant cover, which holds the soil together, is destroyed. The soil becomes exposed and can then be blown or washed away.

Sustainable development: Using the earth's resources in everyday life, while at the same time taking care that the earth can renew those natural resources successfully.

Zoologist: Someone who studies the physical make-up of animals, their habits and characteristics, while also looking at their *habitat*.

Index

Agroforestry 40-42
Antarctica
    ban on mineral prospecting on 53-54
    development of 53
        campaign for a World Park 54
    geography of 52-53

Bernhard, Prince
    and "The 1001: A Nature Trust" 55-56
Biological diversity 58-59

CFCs **63**
Convention on International Trade in Endangered Species of Wild Fauna and Flora (CITES) 23
Chi-Chi 10-11
Cousteau, Jacques 54

Earth Summit 57-59
Elephants
    poaching of 5-7, 19

Global warming 7, 44-46, 49, 58

Huxley, Sir Julian 8-9, 12

International Union for the Conservation of Nature and Natural Resources (IUCN) 8-9, 14, 24, 57
    and the Morges Manifesto 12
International Whaling Commission (IWC)
    founding of 29
    and moratorium on whaling 30
Ivory
    poaching of 5, 7, 19
    smuggling of 22

Logging 34, 38

Medicine
    use of animal parts for 19, 25, 28
"Mission for the 1990s" 56-57
Morges Manifesto 12

"Operation Panda" 30-32
"Operation Tiger" 14, 19, 32

Pandas
    "Operation Panda" 30-32
    Sir Peter Scott and 11, 30-31
Poaching 5, 7, 8, 13, 18-19, 24-26, 32
    prevention of 20-23
"Project Tiger" 16-19
    Indira Gandhi and 16

Rainforest *see also*
    agroforestry 40-41
    deforestation of and logging of 8, 34-35, 37-38, 43
    effect of on local communities 37-39
    importance of 34-35
    protection of 32, 41-42, 46
Ramsar Convention 50
Rhinoceros
    black 19, 23-24
    dehorning of 27-28
    demand for horn of 19, 23-28
    poaching of 13, 23-26

Scott, Sir Peter 9, 11-12, 30-31
Soil erosion 35, 59, **63**
Stolan, Victor 9
Sustainable development 40, 60, **63**
Swan, Robert 54

Tigers
    hunting of 14-15, 19-20
    "Operation Tiger" 14
    "Project Tiger" 16-18, 19
    protection of 14, 16, 18
    tracking of 16-17
Trade Records Analysis of Flora and Fauna in Commerce (TRAFFIC) 20, 22-23, 26

United Nations Environment Programme (UNEP) 57

Wetlands 46-51
    importance of 46-47
    Kafue Flats 48-49
    Mangroves 47, 51, **63**
    Ramsar Convention for the protection of 50-51

Whales
    hunting of 20, 28-30
    ban imposed by IWC 30
Wildlife
    markets for 7, 20, 22-23
    poaching of 5, 7, 8, 13, 18-19, 24-26, 32
    use of for medicines 19, 25, 28
    WWF protection plan for 8
WWF
    and agroforestry 40-42
    change of direction 39-40
    education and training schemes 7, 18, 28, 39, 41-42, 57, 60
    funding of 13-14, 55-56
    and global warming 7, 44-46, 49, 58, **63**
    headquarters of 13
    launch of 12-13
    logo 10-12
    and "Mission for the 1990s" 56-57
    "Operation Panda" 30-32
    "Operation Tiger" 14
    origin of 8-10
    and rhino campaign 23-24
        dehorning 27-28
    role of 7
    "Save the Jungle" campaign 32, 34
    success of 54, 60
    and sustainable development policy 7, 40, 42, 46, 56, 60, **63**
    and the World Conservation Strategy 39
    twentieth birthday of 31
    twenty-fifth anniversary of 54
Wildlife protection plan 8
World Bank, the 43
World Conservation Strategy 39
World Conservation Union *see* IUCN

Yanoama tribe, the 37-39